The Caterpillar Story

Acknowledgments
Executive Editor: Diane Sharpe
Supervising Editor: Stephanie Muller
Design Manager: Sharon Golden
Page Design: Simon Balley Design Associates
Photography: Heather Angel: pages 7, 11; NHPA: cover (top right),
page 28; Natural Science Photos: cover (middle left), pages 12-13,
15, 17, 19, 21, 23, 25, 27, 29.

ISBN 0-8114-3708-6

The Caterpillar Story

Alex Ramsay and Paul Humphrey

Illustrated by
Katy Sleight

STECK-VAUGHN
COMPANY
ELEMENTARY • SECONDARY • ADULT • LIBRARY

They are young caterpillars.

Yes, but you must take care of it.

I'll bring in some
of the leaves you
found it on.

11

My caterpillar has many legs.

They help it cling to the
plants it eats.

My caterpillar is four weeks old now. Look how it has grown.

14

As a caterpillar grows, it changes its skin.

Now my caterpillar is five weeks old. It's much bigger.

16

It has eaten so many leaves.

18

It has started to change. Just wait and watch.

19

20

It has turned into a chrysalis.
What happens next is very
exciting.

21

22

Look what's coming out!

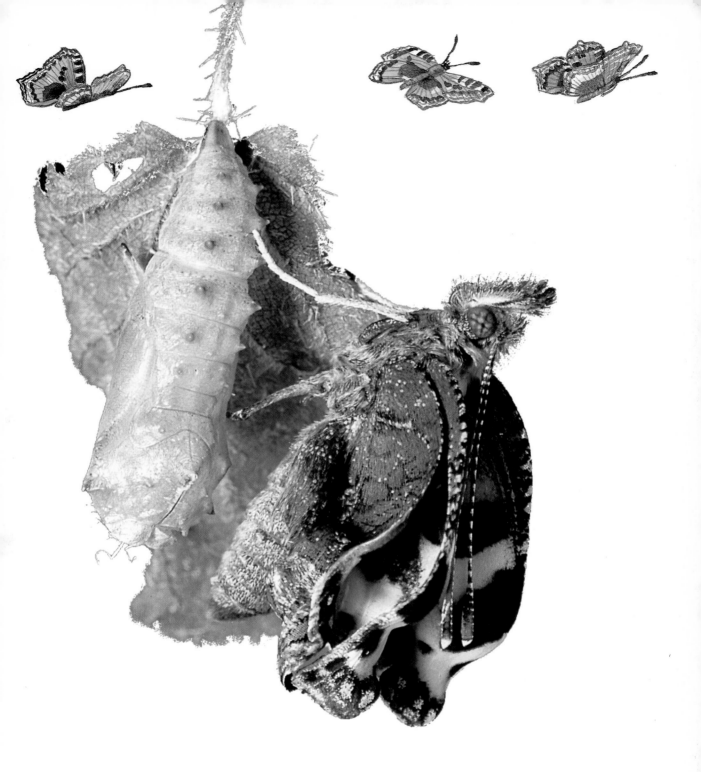

Yes, and now it is drying its wings
in the sunshine.

It's ready to fly away now.
Open the window.

27

It's going outside to find some flowers. Soon it will lay eggs. What will come out of the eggs?

28

More caterpillars will come out!

29

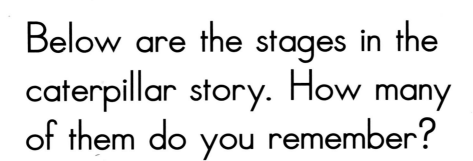

Below are the stages in the caterpillar story. How many of them do you remember?